For Beatrix and Midge, my favorite obstacles — B.E.

Text and illustrations © 2023 Bambi Edlund

Published in Canada and the U.S. by Kids Can Press Ltd.
25 Dockside Drive, Toronto, ON M5A 0B5

Kids Can Press is a Corus Entertainment Inc. company.

www.kidscanpress.com

The artwork in this book was rendered in Adobe Fresco.
The text is set in Avenir LT Std and Meatloaf Solid.

Edited by Jennifer Stokes and Kathleen Fraser
Designed by Michael Reis

Printed and bound in Malaysia, in 3/2023

CM 23 0 9 8 7 6 5 4 3 2 1

Library and Archives Canada Cataloguing in Publication

Title: Operation cupcake : how simple machines work / by Bambi Edlund.
Names: Edlund, Bambi, author, illustrator.
Description: Includes index.
Identifiers: Canadiana (print) 20220459738 | Canadiana (ebook) 20220459762 | ISBN 9781525306679 (hardcover) | ISBN 9781525308215 (EPUB)
Subjects: LCSH: Simple machines — Juvenile literature.
Classification: LCC TJ147 .E35 2023 | DDC j621.8 — dc23

Kids Can Press gratefully acknowledges that the land on which our office is located is the traditional territory of many nations, including the Mississaugas of the Credit, the Anishnabeg, the Chippewa, the Haudenosaunee and the Wendat peoples, and is now home to many diverse First Nations, Inuit and Métis peoples.

We thank the Government of Ontario, through Ontario Creates; the Ontario Arts Council; the Canada Council for the Arts; and the Government of Canada for supporting our publishing activity.

OPERATION CUPCAKE

How Simple Machines Work

by Bambi Edlund

KIDS CAN PRESS

the **TARGET**

An especially aromatic vanilla cupcake with pink buttercream frosting and sprinkles, baked fresh this morning.

the **TEAM**

GINGERSNAP

A smart cookie who always has an action plan. Ginger loves nothing more than a challenging problem that needs solving — except maybe a buttercream frosting that needs eating.

MACAROON

Mac is a trusty sidekick, always eager to lend a hand in carrying out his sister Ginger's plans. His favorite activities are (in order) feasting, snacking and munching.

the **MISSION**

Use simple machines to bring the cupcake home. Ginger and Mac live in a cozy little mousehole under the stairs, conveniently close to the kitchen. When the humans go out, they snap into action, collecting delicious treats and whisking them home. This morning, however, their treat of choice is too large to pick up and carry across the kitchen, so they will need to use simple machines to get the job done.

the **OBSTACLES**

High things, heavy things, hard-to-move things. Also a perpetually crabby, eagle-eyed cat and an overly enthusiastic, always hungry dog. Plus time, because the humans will be returning home soon!

the SIX SIMPLE MACHINES

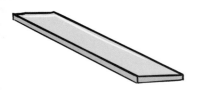

INCLINED PLANE

A ramp that helps when moving an object between lower and higher locations.

LEVER

A bar connected to a pivot point (called a fulcrum) that helps move heavy objects.

PULLEY

A wheel and a rope that, used together, make lifting heavy objects easier.

WHEEL AND AXLE

A wheel and attached center rod that rotate together to help to move heavy things long distances.

SCREW

A raised ridge wrapped around a cylinder that helps to hold things together or lift and lower an object.

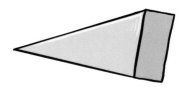

WEDGE

A tool that tapers to a thin or sharp edge and helps to split something or to keep objects in place.

If we have to climb up high or lift something heavy or cut something in two, simple machines make it easier.

Okay ... as long as we get that cupcake!

FORCE

Force is the effort needed to pull or push an object. Anytime you make something move, you are applying force. Forces make things move, speed up, slow down or stop.

WORK

Work is the use of force to move an object. When you use energy (move your muscles) to apply force to a task, for example, lifting, pushing, pulling or otherwise moving an object, that is considered work.

WHAT IS A SIMPLE MACHINE?

Any tool used to help you move something is a machine. This includes obvious things, such as cars and computers and can openers, but did you know your toothbrush is actually a machine? So is a pencil, a tennis racket and a knife. They all make doing something easier. Even parts of your body are machines!

Simple machines, such as a shovel or a baseball bat or a nail, are machines that do one thing. They have few or no moving parts. Things such as bicycles, scissors and wheelbarrows are complex machines, because they are made of two or more simple machines working together, with moving parts.

The six simple machines help us to push, pull, lift and divide. They help us cut things, move things and reach things that are far away. Machines give us a mechanical advantage. That means they make doing work easier than it would be without the aid of machines.

Imagine trying to get a nail into a piece of wood without a hammer or gathering a lot of leaves without a rake.

There are trade-offs to all of this help we get from simple machines. Using pulleys to pull something heavy up into the air means we don't have to strain our backs trying to lift it, but we do have to pull the rope down a greater distance than the heavy object is raised. Putting in less effort over a greater distance is usually a good trade-off. That's why we use simple machines so often.

10

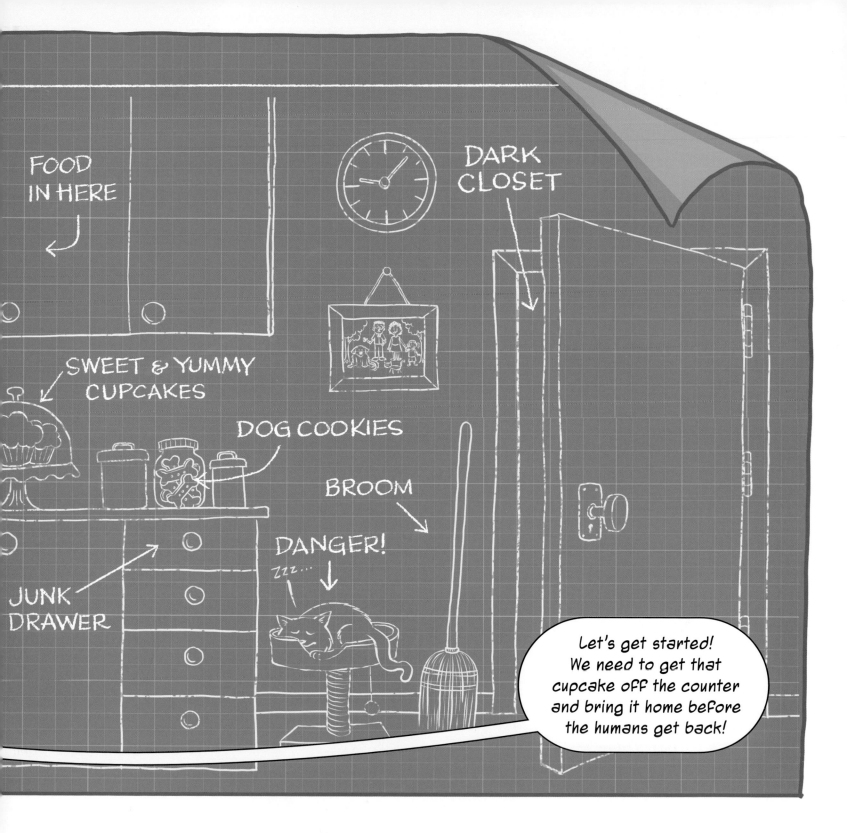

SIMPLE MACHINE #1
THE INCLINED PLANE

An inclined plane is a flat surface that is raised at one end so it slopes. Wheelchair ramps, playground slides, hilly roads and even stairs are all inclined planes.

When moving an object (or a mouse) from a lower level to a higher one, it is much easier to use an inclined plane than it is to climb straight up. The trade-off is that you have to walk a longer distance to get there.

An inclined plane is also useful when lowering a heavy object. The friction between the object and the ramp slows the object, so it's easier to lower. Again, the trade-off is you have to move it farther.

14

COMMON INCLINED PLANES

ramps

staircases

slides

escalators

conveyor belts

ladders

mountain roads

Yay! We made it!

We sure did!

Can we throw the ball for the dog again?

Not now, Mac. Next, we have to lift that dome ...

CLAP!

IMPORTANT TERMS

FRICTION

Friction is a force that slows movement when an object moves across a surface. Friction causes resistance. The rougher the surface, the more resistance there is. Think about sliding across a smooth floor in your socks, then imagine trying to slide across pavement. Pavement is much rougher, so there is more resistance, causing your socks to stick rather than slide.

Friction is an important part of using an inclined plane. If you are lowering a heavy object, you might want more friction to keep the object from moving too quickly, such as a ramp that has no-slip strips so you don't slide. But if you are pushing an object up a ramp, you may want less friction so it can move more easily.

TRY IT OUT

MAKE AN INCLINED PLANE

You will need:

- a plank of wood or other board
- some books
- a small toy car
- a paper cup or empty yogurt container
- a pen or a small screwdriver
- coins or marbles
- a strip of fabric

1. Place a piece of wood with one end on a stack of books, near the edge of a table.

2. Tie a piece of string that is longer than the ramp around the toy car, from back to front, and knot it near the front. Use a pen or small screwdriver to punch two small holes on opposite sides of the paper cup or yogurt container near the rim, then run the other end of the string through the holes and tie it above the container.

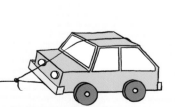 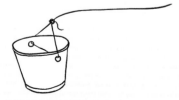

3. Place the car at the bottom of the ramp and hang the cup over the top end of the ramp. Drop coins into the cup one at a time. See how many coins it takes to make the car roll up the ramp.

4. Now put more books under the ramp so it's steeper. Does it take more or fewer coins to make the car move?

ADD SOME FRICTION

5. Try taping some fabric to the board. How many coins do you need to make the car drive now?

On a seesaw, we take turns being the force or the load.

SIMPLE MACHINE #2
THE LEVER

A lever is a rigid rod or bar that connects to a fulcrum, which is the pivot or turning point. (Rigid means it won't bend. You can't use a wet noodle as a lever.) Using a lever means you need less effort to move an object. You have to pull or push the lever a greater distance than you would have to move the object, but the effort you have to make is easier and takes less energy.

A seesaw is a good example of a lever. If you tried to lift someone larger than you using only your arms, it would be difficult. But you can move them on a seesaw because the lever makes the work of lifting them much easier.

There are three kinds of levers, with the fulcrum in different locations for each.

COMMON LEVERS

chopsticks

hammers

crowbars

spoons

baseball bats

bottle openers

can openers

rakes

CLASS 1 LEVER

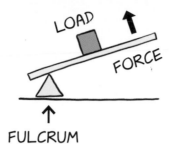

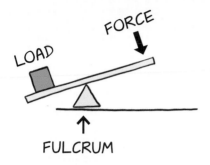

CLASS 2 LEVER

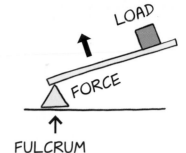

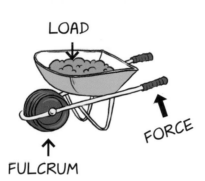

CLASS 3 LEVER

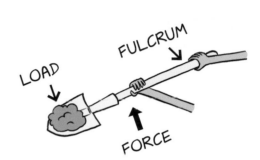

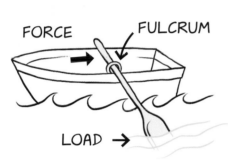

A boat oar is a Class 1 lever, with the fulcrum in between the load (water) and the force (your arm). If you hold an oar at the top end only and try to push through the water, it's nearly impossible. But if you use the oar as a lever (with the oarlock as the fulcrum), it's much easier.

A wheelbarrow is a Class 2 lever, with the fulcrum at one end (the wheel), the force at the other end (your arms lifting up the handles) and the load in the middle (in the bucket). If you try lifting the bucket, it's very heavy, but if you use the handles, it is much easier.

A shovel is a Class 3 lever, with the fulcrum at one end (one hand holding the end of the handle), the load at the other end (in the spade of the shovel) and the force in the middle (your other hand pushing up on the handle). If you try lifting a full shovel straight up with both hands, it's much more difficult than using it as a lever.

When Ginger used a spatula to open the drawer, the fulcrum was the edge of the counter, the load was the drawer and the force was Ginger pulling the handle.

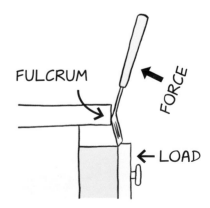

Remember the string we found in the junk drawer?

String? How will we use that?

It's going to help us lift that heavy lid.

First, we need to get up on that shelf. To do that, we need to make a catapult!

TRY IT OUT

MAKE YOUR OWN CATAPULT!

You will need:

- a long wooden dowel or wooden spoon with a round handle
- a pipe cleaner
- a large soupspoon or serving spoon
- two heavy objects, such as books or bags of rice
- a small pom-pom or a marshmallow
- a beanbag

1. Twist both ends of the pipe cleaner around the wooden spoon handle, making a small arch in the center.

2. Place the wooden spoon on a table with the flat side down.

3. Rest the two heavy objects on either end of the wooden spoon to hold it in place.

4. Push the handle of the soupspoon through the pipe cleaner.

5. Put the pom-pom in the soupspoon.

6. Drop the beanbag on the opposite end of the spoon to launch your pom-pom!

7. Try moving the spoon so the fulcrum is in different locations and see how much farther the pom-pom travels when the fulcrum is closer to the end of the spoon or farther away.

What type of lever do you think this is: Class 1, Class 2 or Class 3?

THE CATAPULT

A catapult is a Class 1 lever. Here, the ladle is the lever, Mac is the load and Ginger's body weight is the force.

Ginger jumping on the end of the ladle will propel Mac up onto the shelf, but only if the fulcrum is in the proper place.

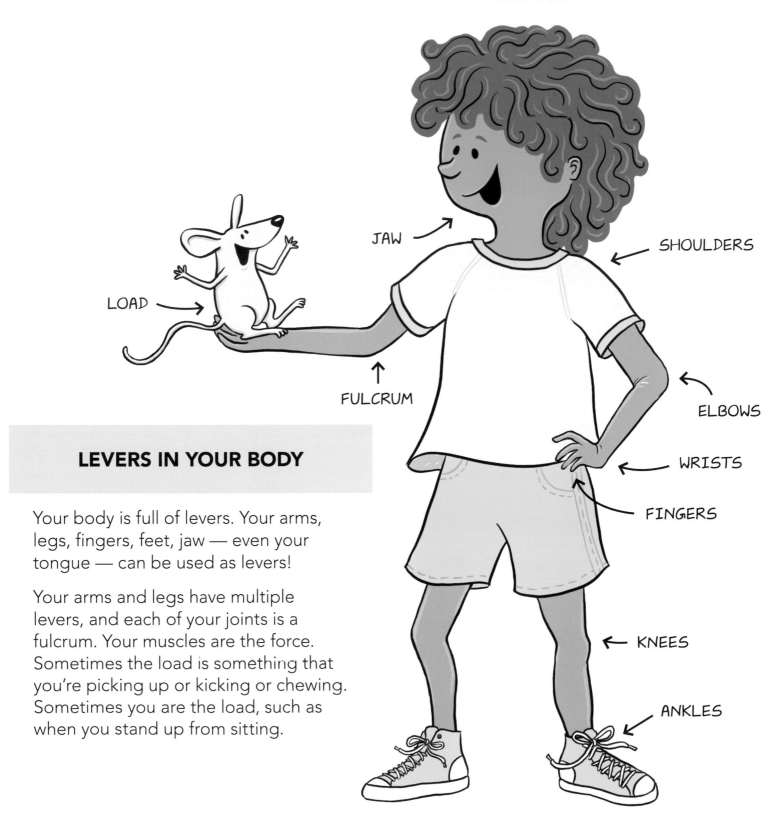

JAW

SHOULDERS

LOAD

FULCRUM

ELBOWS

WRISTS

FINGERS

KNEES

ANKLES

LEVERS IN YOUR BODY

Your body is full of levers. Your arms, legs, fingers, feet, jaw — even your tongue — can be used as levers!

Your arms and legs have multiple levers, and each of your joints is a fulcrum. Your muscles are the force. Sometimes the load is something that you're picking up or kicking or chewing. Sometimes you are the load, such as when you stand up from sitting.

TRY IT OUT

TEST YOUR ARM LEVER

You will need:

- a small ball, such as a tennis ball or baseball

BEND ONLY
AT WRIST

BEND ONLY
AT ELBOW

BEND AT
SHOULDER

1. Try throwing a ball bending your arm only at your wrist and mark how far it goes.

2. Next, try it using only the lower part of your arm, bending at your elbow, and mark how far it goes this time.

3. Now try using your entire arm by moving your shoulder and keeping the rest of your arm straight. How far does it go?

Have you ever seen someone using a ball-launcher with a long handle to throw a ball for their dog? The handle allows them to extend their arm lever even farther!

SIMPLE MACHINE #3
THE PULLEY

A pulley is a wheel with a rope that runs over it. Usually the wheel has a groove along its edge to guide the rope. It is used to help lift objects more easily by changing the direction of the force needed. This means that if you want to lift something heavy upward, you have to pull the rope downward, in the opposite direction from where you want the heavy object to go! The trade-off is that you must pull the rope a greater distance, but it's much easier than lifting something heavy straight up.

The more pulleys you use, the easier the lifting becomes, but the farther you have to pull. If you had enough pulleys and a lot of rope, you could lift a car by yourself!

COMMON PULLEYS

cranes

flagpole pulley

sailboat rigging

clothesline

weight-lifting equipment

25

MAKE A PULLEY

You will need:

- a broom handle or similar round pole

- two surfaces of equal height (to place the pole across)

- a rope about 3 m (10 ft.) long

- a large plastic jug with a handle and a lid

1. Place a broom handle or a similar round pole across two stable surfaces of the same height, such as a table and a countertop. This will act as your pulley wheel.

2. Tie a rope to the handle of a large jug filled with water or a jug of laundry detergent.

3. First, hold the rope and try lifting the jug straight up.

4. Now try looping the rope over the broom handle to create a pulley. Sit on the floor and pull the rope downward to lift the jug. You use the same amount of force, but it is usually easier to pull down than to lift up, especially when you want to raise an object above your head where you can't reach.

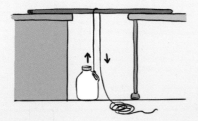

5. Now loop the rope through the jug handle and over the broom once more and pull down. Then loop it once more. You need to use more rope and to pull the rope a greater distance with each additional pulley, but notice how much easier it is to lift the jug when you are using more pulleys.

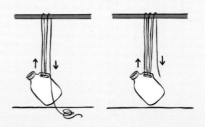

27

SIMPLE MACHINE #4
WHEEL AND AXLE

A wheel and axle is made of two round objects, usually a larger wheel that rotates with a smaller rod (axle) attached in the center. When used for transport (such as on a car or wagon), a wheel and axle helps to reduce friction, making it easier to move heavy objects.

A wheel and axle also makes it easier to turn things by increasing the mechanical advantage. A faucet is a wheel and axle that makes turning on the tap much easier.

COMMON WHEELS AND AXLES

pizza cutters

doorknobs

roller skates

car wheels

fans

faucets

rolling pins

MAKE A WHEEL AND AXLE

You will need:

- two chopsticks, wooden skewers or similar thin rods

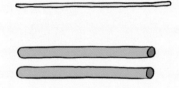

- two drinking straws (wide enough to fit the rods)

- a small box (make sure the box is narrower than the length of the chopsticks) or a toilet paper tube

- four wheels — you could cut round wheels from cardboard or use large buttons (all four should be the same size)

- tape or glue

- scissors

1. Cut each straw so it's a little wider than the box or toilet paper tube (the body of the car) and tape or glue a straw across each end of the bottom of the car.

2. Glue or tape one wheel to one end of each thin rod (axle). Make sure the axle is in the very center of the wheel.

3. Feed the axles through the straws and attach the remaining two wheels.

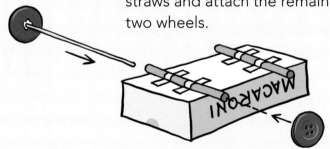

WHY ADD WHEELS?

ROLLING VERSUS DRAGGING

Wheels on a wagon make it easier to pull because only the edge of each wheel makes contact with the ground. That means there is less friction than if you were dragging the wagon across the ground. Because the wheels turn freely rather than slide across the surface, friction is reduced.

IMPORTANT TERMS

PUSHING AND PULLING

There are two types of force: pushing and pulling. A pull is a force moving something toward you. A push is a force moving something away from you. When both forces are used, the effort is shared. With Ginger pushing and Mac pulling the car, it takes less effort to move the cupcake home!

How can one little screw be a machine?

It helps to pull one thing toward another!

SIMPLE MACHINE #5
THE SCREW

Screws help to hold things together tightly. They also help to move objects (and people!) up and down more easily.

A screw is an inclined plane wrapped around a cylinder. Remember, an inclined plane helps move an object from a lower level to a higher one, but the object has to travel a longer distance. Imagine you need to climb up something very high, such as a lighthouse, and there isn't room for a long ramp. If the ramp is wrapped around the lighthouse, it still gives the same mechanical advantage as using a straight ramp, but without it having to stretch from a long, long ways away!

A jar lid is a type of screw. Turning it around the neck of a jar moves it up or down, opening or closing the jar.

HOW A SCREW WORKS

Here's an easy way to see how a screw can help with a long climb.

You will need:

- a piece of paper

- a crayon, colored pencil or marker

- a long cardboard tube (such as an empty paper towel tube)

1. Cut the paper on a diagonal in the shape of a triangle so it makes a long ramp.

2. Color a line along the long edge of the paper (the top of the ramp).

3. Place the cardboard tube on one of the uncolored edges of the paper and roll the paper around it.

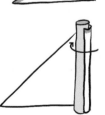

You will see how your ramp now wraps around the tube in a spiral.

If this were a road, you would still travel the same distance as when the paper was flat, and at the same angle, but you could start at the bottom of the mountain, instead of two towns over!

SIMPLE MACHINE #6
THE WEDGE

A wedge is two inclined planes joined together. It is thicker on one end, and usually forms a sharp edge on the other end.

Wedges are used to cut things or split them apart, or to hold things together. The sharper the tip of a wedge is, the easier it is to push through the object being cut. A longer wedge requires less force because it has a narrower tip, and a shorter wedge requires more force because it has a wider tip.

Wedges often have handles that act as levers, making the work of splitting things easier. An ax is a wedge with a handle. Adding the lever (handle) makes splitting wood much easier, because the handle increases the force. Pushing an ax without a handle through a piece of wood would take far more effort.

COMMON WEDGES

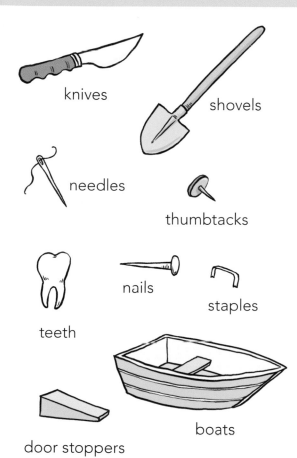

knives

shovels

needles

thumbtacks

teeth

nails

staples

boats

door stoppers

A WEDGE IN ACTION

You will need:

- a block of cheese or cold butter

- a butter knife

- a cutting board

1. Unwrap the cheese and place it on the cutting board.

2. Place the knife blade flat on top of the cheese and try pushing down. Does it cut through the cheese?

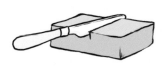

3. Try using the handle of the knife to push through the cheese. Does this split it?

4. Now turn the knife so the narrowest edge (the wedge) is on top of the cheese and push down. Does this split the cheese in two?

Throw me the ball of string, Mac! But hang on to the other end.

I'll loop it around this doorknob ...

Now you cut the end using your own wedges ... your teeth!

COMPLEX MACHINES

Complex machines consist of two or more simple machines working together, with moving parts. Some complex machines use only two simple machines, and some use dozens!

SCISSORS

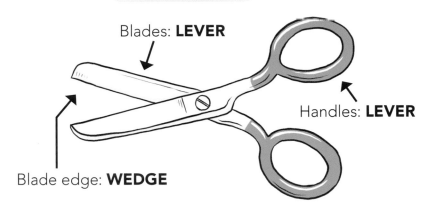

Blades: **LEVER**

Handles: **LEVER**

Blade edge: **WEDGE**

BICYCLE

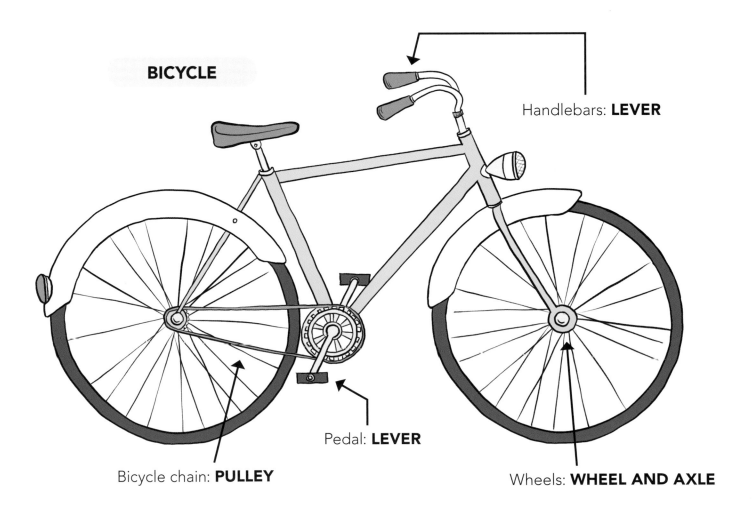

Handlebars: **LEVER**

Pedal: **LEVER**

Bicycle chain: **PULLEY**

Wheels: **WHEEL AND AXLE**

COMMON COMPLEX MACHINES

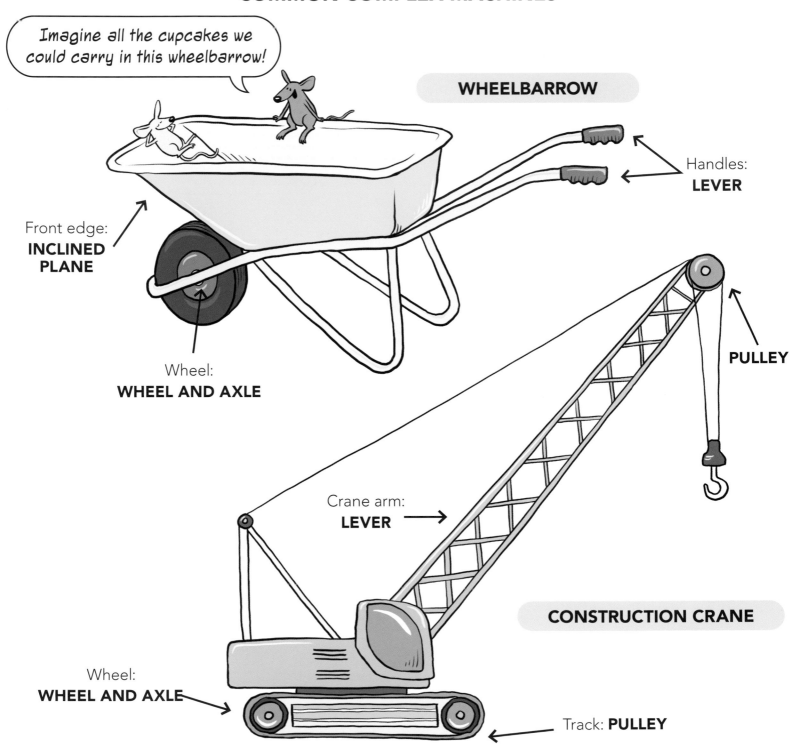

Imagine all the cupcakes we could carry in this wheelbarrow!

WHEELBARROW

Handles: **LEVER**

Front edge: **INCLINED PLANE**

Wheel: **WHEEL AND AXLE**

PULLEY

Crane arm: **LEVER**

CONSTRUCTION CRANE

Wheel: **WHEEL AND AXLE**

Track: **PULLEY**

FISHING ROD

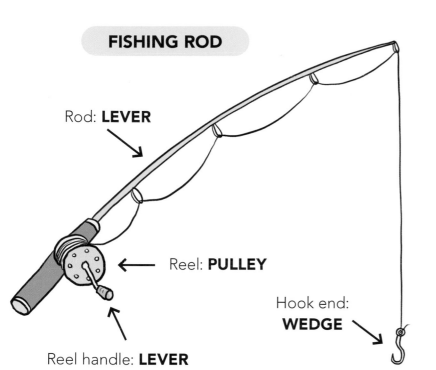

Rod: **LEVER**

Reel: **PULLEY**

Reel handle: **LEVER**

Hook end: **WEDGE**

CAN OPENER

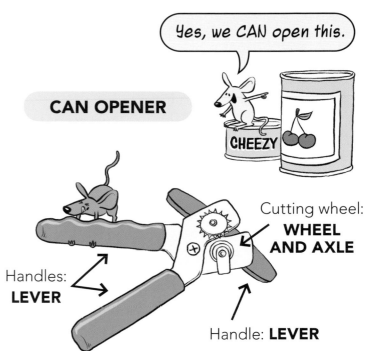

Yes, we CAN open this.

CHEEZY

Cutting wheel: **WHEEL AND AXLE**

Handles: **LEVER**

Handle: **LEVER**

CORKSCREW

Arms: **LEVER**

SCREW

MOTORBOAT

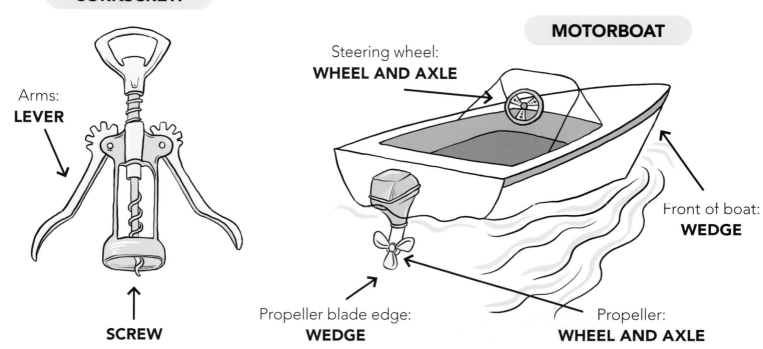

Steering wheel: **WHEEL AND AXLE**

Front of boat: **WEDGE**

Propeller blade edge: **WEDGE**

Propeller: **WHEEL AND AXLE**

41

GLOSSARY

axle: a rigid rod or bar connected to the center of a wheel

catapult: a device that uses a lever to help propel objects through the air

complex machine: a machine comprised of two or more simple machines working together

cylinder: an object with flat circular ends and straight sides

effort: the physical energy used to do something

force: the effort needed to move an object

friction: a force that causes resistance between the surfaces of objects

fulcrum: the point on which a lever rests, pivots or turns

inclined plane: a sloping flat surface that helps when moving an object between lower and higher locations

lever: a rigid bar that, when connected to a pivot point (called a fulcrum), helps to move objects

load: an object being moved

machine: an object used to apply mechanical power to help perform a task

mechanical advantage: the amount of help you get by using a simple machine

pivot: the point on which an object turns

pulley: a device made of a wheel and a rope that together make lifting heavy objects easier by changing the direction of the force needed

ramp: a sloped surface or inclined plane joining two different levels

resistance: a force that slows movement

rigid: stiff and unbending

screw: an inclined plane with raised ridges wrapped around a cylinder that helps to lift and lower an object or hold things together

simple machine: a machine that does one thing, with few or no moving parts

task: some work to be done

trade-off: giving up one thing to get another, for example, walking a greater distance up a long ramp rather than climbing straight up

wedge: a tool that tapers to a thin or sharp edge and helps to cut or split something or to hold together or keep objects in place

wheel: a circular disk that revolves with a smaller axle, used to move an object more easily

wheel and axle: a wheel and attached center rod that rotate together to help to move heavy things long distances

work: the transfer of energy that happens when you apply any force to a task, for example, lifting, pushing, pulling or otherwise moving an object

INDEX

axles, 8, 28–30

catapults, 20, 21

complex machines, 9, 36–39

dragging versus rolling, 30

force, 9, 19, 21, 22, 26, 31, 34

friction, 13, 15, 16, 28, 30

fulcrum, 8, 18–22

inclined planes, 8, 10–16, 33, 34

   list of common examples, 15

   make one, 16

levers, 8, 17–23

   as part of wedges, 34

   in your body, 22, 23

   list of common examples, 18

   make one, 20

   three classes of, 19

load, 19, 21, 22

mechanical advantage, 9, 28, 33

pivot point, 8, 18. *See also* fulcrum

pulleys, 8, 24–26, 37

   list of common examples, 24

   make one, 26

pushing and pulling, 9, 31

ramps, 8, 13, 15, 16, 33. *See also* inclined
    planes

resistance, 15. *See also* friction

rolling versus dragging, 30

screws, 8, 32–33

   how they work, 33

simple machines

   definition, 9

   list of six, 8

trade-offs, 9, 13, 24

wedges, 8, 34–35

   list of common examples, 35

   use one, 35

wheels, 8, 24, 26, 28–30

wheels and axles, 8, 28–30

   list of common examples, 28

   make one, 30

work, 9, 13